T0128396

Dr. Rosita Cantu

Naomi's Hope

WESTBOW
P R E S S®
A DIVISION OF THOMAS NELSON
& ZONDERVAN

WestBow Press books may be ordered through booksellers or by contacting:

WestBow Press
A Division of Thomas Nelson & Zondervan
1663 Liberty Drive
Bloomington, IN 47403
www.westbowpress.com
1 (866) 928-1240

ISBN: 978-1-9736-7844-1 (sc)
ISBN: 978-1-9736-7845-8 (e)

Library of Congress Control Number: 2019917807

Print information available on the last page.

WestBow Press rev. date: 11/04/2019

I dedicate this book to my husband, daughter, and son. I love you!

Contents

Preface

Bitter horseradish is very bitter. I found that out in a hurry when I dipped my Chinese egg roll in the bowl, and it left a bitter aftertaste. I will never do that again. Naomi, the main character of the book of Ruth, did not see herself as pleasant at all. She changed her name to reflect her bitter life. She looked at her bleak situation and saw her true colors. The word *bitter* is a strong word that refers to her personal dilemmas while in a strange town called Moab in the time of the judges, a perilous time for the nation of Israel.

The transition—her move from Bethlehem to Moab—was not beneficial because she lost her husband, two sons, and any possible chance of grandchildren and a daughter-in-law. What did she have to offer to anyone?

I wrote this book to provide hope and healing for the grieving mother, father, daughter, aunt, uncle, niece, nephew, sister, brother, and fiancé.

I pray it will encourage every US Marine family involved in Operation Iraqi Freedom. I believe it will bring encouragement to those who have lost everything.

After my last bout with illness, I contacted another friend who was an author and said, "It is time to write *Naomi's Hope*." I felt a sense of urgency to write this book but could not because of grief. Later in the year, I became ill again. I called my friend's daughter, a possible publisher for *Naomi's Hope*. I had hoped to submit a manuscript to her, but it was delayed even more.

I preached *Naomi's Hope* twice in my local church, and the first sermon was even recorded. *Naomi's Hope* developed from my experience grieving for my son. This book comes from my heart as I share my hopelessness and how God brought restoration to my life. There is hope for the hopeless!

Introduction

This note is for the readers of my book. I am a Christian who loves the Lord with all my heart, soul, and mind. I lost my son. I offer my condolences and prayers for your own losses. May you and your families be comforted in the Holy Spirit. I have prayed for you as my readers.

How to Get the Most from This Book

1. Read a chapter a week.
2. Meditate upon the topic and the scriptures of each chapter.
3. Reflect upon the author's notes and their correlation to the main topic of each chapter.
4. Focus on the reader's notes section in each chapter as well. These are the parts of the book where you, the reader, will have an opportunity to interact directly with the content. Please feel free to write in the book or in your journal.

chapter 1

Way Too Much Grief!

Even if I thought there was still hope ...
—Ruth 1:12

In Naomi's thoughts, there was no hope for future sons to marry her daughters-in-law; she was past the reproduction stage. Naomi spoke to her daughters-in-law to persuade them to go home. The book of Ruth shows the hopelessness of Naomi's situation. It teaches the believer how to identify losses, events, changes, transitions, or triggers that can cause grief.

The famine affected everything. She moved from her home, family, and friends in Bethlehem (Ruth 1:1). The family relocated to Moab for a higher standard of living. The harvest provided employment and groceries. Life was simply better in Moab!

The definition of loss is losing someone through death, a broken relationship, or separation by distance or divorce. Loss can even refer to material things, such a brand-new car that is involved in a wreck. In life, certain events, changes, or transitions are stressful, including moves, deaths, relationships, marriage, and change of job, career, or education. For example, an individual can grieve over a loved one who is with the Lord, a wrecked car, a broken relationship, a dream home demolished, sickness, depleted savings and retirement accounts, lack of promotion, or a career that never happens. Our loved ones in the Lord are not lost. They are found because they are with Jesus in heaven.

The first loss Naomi experienced was the home where her children were born and raised and where she labored to provide meals. It was cozy and comfortable. As the home administrator, she grew a garden, made clothes, handled the finances, and performed the other tasks it took to run an efficient home.

The famine brought insecurity and transition for Naomi and many other women in Bethlehem. Many husbands made decisions to secure the future of their families. Naomi prepared for the change. The exchange of good-byes overwhelmed her. She left behind family and friends.

It was not long before Naomi experienced a second loss: the death of her husband, Elimelech, the father of her children. How unfortunate for it to have occurred in the first year of their arrival in a strange land (Ruth 1:3). His name meant "God of the king." She had relied upon him for love, affirmation, direction, guidance, and the well-being of her family. Naomi trusted him in any decision he made for the family and believed it was for the good. But now she was alone, a widow.

Misfortune visited Naomi for the third time when she experienced the death of her firstborn, Mahlon, which means "sickly." He died after ten years in Moab (Ruth 1:4–5). Mahlon passed away on a fine, lovely morning while he was working in the family workshop. His survivors included his mother, Naomi; his wife, Orpah; his brother, Chilion; and his sister-in-law, Ruth. Unfortunately, Mahlon and Orpah were married and without children, a fourth loss. Now she was a widow like Naomi.

Life continued, and Chilion, which means "pining," was the head of the household. Naomi still enjoyed the company of her baby boy. Now he was a grown man with a beautiful wife named Ruth, a Moabite. Unfortunately, Naomi was infatuated with her baby boy, just as any mother or father. She did not know that she would experience death for a fifth time. Chilion and Ruth were childless, the sixth loss. The widow's web grew. Ruth was now a part of it.

Naomi received the news that the famine was over in Bethlehem. It was time to leave Moab, one more transition and the seventh loss (Ruth 1:6–7). Naomi did not hesitate to make the trip, so she made her plans. What is this? Is it another loss? She may have thought, *The famine continues, so is it still in the best interest of the family to stay in Moab?* After her sons died, there was no hope for the birth of a son or sons to wed the daughters-in-law, so she told them to return to their homes. Orpah returned to her home, which was another change. Naomi wondered when she would see her again. Would their relationship be lost (an eighth loss)?

Naomi and Ruth walked toward Bethlehem. Ten years of memories included a spouse's funeral and maybe some bliss with two weddings. However, the brides were not Israelites, and that was probably disappointing to Naomi, but she may have finally accepted them (ninth and tenth losses, but who was counting?) and way too much grief!

Author's Notes

What else could happen to Naomi? She had lost it all!

I was there. I have lost it all, or at least I've felt like it. In seven years, I lost my son, brother, mother, and father. My family moved several times during my last thirty years of marriage because of the ministry. Decisions were made, and we moved from one town to another. Then, before I knew it, we moved again and again.

We all experienced the moving transition, as we left behind family and friends. My son cried at night. Both children needed new clothes. The financial pressure overwhelmed our family, and tension mounted.

Everyone adjusted when it came time to move again, including to a new school. This time it was cell phones and sports cars. How do you explain to your friends that you live on a Bible school campus (your parents are the faculty) in a dorm that was remodeled into a home? Welcome to the biggest and most influential high school in San Antonio, Texas! The other students' parents were probably doctors and engineers. Peer pressure was unmerciful to my children.

Naomi lost those dearest to her. I lost my baby son, and that was too much to bear, but she lost two. Barbara Johnson, a speaker for the Women of Faith organization, shared about how she lost two sons and overcame through laughter. She has since passed away and is with the Lord and her sons. Just the thought of my husband's death was enough to send me to the grief counselor. It seemed like a never-ending cycle of death and grief, the thought of death and what could happen next. Death and then grief and then another blow! The mind replayed like a tape recorder loop. Everything was consumed with death and grief! My spirit was strong, but my mind did not know what to think. My emotions went haywire, and my brain tilted. My heart was broken into pieces, and I could not understand why. My body began to shut down to protect the core: my heart and brain. It happened to me!

I thought the grief would pass, but the continual blows that death brought were too much for my mind, emotions, and body. "We have done every possible test, and we cannot find anything wrong with you," the doctor said in the emergency room.

What was wrong with me? I could not speak. I did not

know who I was. I was nameless. My body did not have strength, and I could not stand on my own. My husband carried me to the car. My vision blurred, and the light was too bright. I covered my head with a hood and a blanket, plus I wore my sunglasses. "Lord, the light is too bright," I said as my husband drove me to the emergency room when my vision blurred. "It was not a stroke," the doctors said countless times.

Reader's Notes

Just think about it, write it down, and talk with God about it. Write Him a letter. Ask Him all your questions. He will answer, but you may not like the answers. Take it slow. Breathe in and out.

chapter 2

Oh No! The Tank Is on Empty!

*I went away full, but the Lord has
brought me back empty.*

—Ruth 1:21

Naomi experienced many losses within the last ten years of her life in Moab. I can only imagine how she felt. Her nerves were tattered, and her mind and body were worn from grief. She was not in high spirits concerning her future.

Can this be Naomi?

Her arrival in Bethlehem caused a great stir among the community. Quickly, they saw her ragtag state and questioned, "Can this be Naomi?" (Ruth 1:19). Of course it was! She was different, though. The glimmer in her eyes was not there; her lips quivered when she spoke as tears ran down her cheeks; her face, once youthful, had aged, with lines showing around her eyes and lips; and her posture was bent over.

The community knew Naomi as pleasant when she had lived in Bethlehem at the house on the corner with the beautiful garden full of an array of lilies, zinnias, cosmos, and marigolds and the sweet aromas of basil, rosemary, lavender, and mint. Her front door had been the gateway to a wonderful home, where many came to visit the family. The smells from the kitchen had been amazing as fresh matzos baked and beef stew simmered in a pot. She had welcomed everyone; no one was ever left out. Elimelech had enjoyed the hospitality of his beautiful wife; he was honored by her way of living. She had been a joyful mother of children. Mahlon and Chilion had worked with their father and played with cousins nearby. When their mother called, they had run quickly home. Their mother's home cooking had been the best part of their days.

The women thought, *But she made it back. I thought I would never see her again. But where are Elimelech, Mahlon, and Chilion? By now, they should have married and borne Naomi grandchildren. I do not see them. Will they come later?* Naomi was overwhelmed by the thought of her condition. She felt alone. Her countenance became somber, and her hands gestured discouragement.

Call Me Mara

Naomi quickly changed her name to Mara, which means "bitter and sad" (Ruth 1:20–21). It was a true representation of her life in the hands of God Almighty. In the Old Testament, at the place of Marah, the waters were bitter. Moses threw a palm tree into the water to sweeten it. The people of Bethlehem asked, "What has happened, Naomi? Now you ask us to call you Mara. This new name does not depict your life, Naomi, when we knew you ..."

Naomi acknowledged it was the Almighty who had made her life bitter and that He had his hand upon her (Ruth 1:20). "I buried my husband, Elimelech, "God of the king," a man of the tribe of Judah, from the family of the Hezronites, and a kinsman of Boaz, when we first arrived in Moab, and within ten years, Mahlon and Chilion passed away in the land of Moab. I lost my hope of grandchildren after their deaths. My daughter-in-law Orpah, through my persuasion, returned home. My social standing, security, and hopes for a future are lost."

"The Lord has brought me back empty!" Naomi exclaims (Ruth 1:21). "My family did not make it back with me." Naomi was surreal in her circumstances. Of the original four, it was she. Elimelech was not there to help her through the grief at their sons' deaths or when she had to make the decision to return to Bethlehem.

"The Lord has afflicted me" (Ruth 1:21). Naomi recognized that He had caused her afflictions and that He had not left her alone. She had a covenant relationship with God, who disciplines His own children. God was working in her life for His glory, but she could not see it because of all the tragedies she had experienced.

"The Almighty has brought misfortune upon me" (Ruth 1:21). It was He! God did it to her. What? The women did not say anything back to her like, "Oh, Naomi, you are just exaggerating! I do not see that you came back alone. There is Ruth, your daughter-in-law, and she came with you." Or the women could have said, "God did this to you? Are you sure?

Author's Notes

Saturday, May 8, 2010, 8:00 a.m.

Oh Lord, my God, how I love you and appreciate you. You are an awesome God! Marvelous, wonderful, merciful, and gracious! Oh how you love me. I love you with all my heart and with everything that is within me. Forever, I will love you.

You have given me mercy and grace for my life. You have not forsaken me. I see your mercy in my life and in my garden—the roses, pansies, cyclamen, begonias, lavender, mint, strawberries, impatiens, marigolds, and all the other plants. God, you have given me mercy.

It is hard to let go of school, but I must remind myself that you are in control of my life in 2010 and 2011.

I have mercy from you. Lord, as I stood by the window, working on my plants, the decision had been made to travel to London for the engagement party. I knew that you had spoken to me and given me mercy to travel to London in July 2010, to Deborah's graduation in March 2011, and to the wedding on July 7, 2012.

I understand now what Jesus my Lord went through in the Garden of Gethsemane, "not my will but your will."

The teardrops of blood that fell from His brow to the ground where He prayed. When it was settled, He got up and did the Father's will. Off to the cross He went to make the ultimate sacrifice, the lamb called to the slaughter, silently. His life brought many to Himself.

My son gave his life for his country, family, and friends, and he did not look back. He knew that he might die for us. He was willing to do it. He was willing. My baby was so young, just a boy but also a young man with a grave responsibility upon his shoulders.

I thought about how no one wants to die, grieve, or experience the death of my Lord Jesus Christ, but I am reminded of the saints Paul, who was beheaded; John, who boiled in hot scorching oil; Peter, who was hung upside down on the cross because he did not feel worthy to crucified like my Lord.

My sister got it right. She prepared my mother for her death, and she did it the only way she knew how.

I must not fear death, the opening door, and walking through the other side to see my Lord and Savior Jesus Christ, to see my Heavenly Father, to be ushered into His presence.

I have asked my God not to let me suffer in death but to take me without suffering. Why do I cry these tears? Perhaps they are what I will leave behind. David chose to go be with the Father. Why would he not? He counted the cost; his soul was prepared, and so he went.

I would have gone, too. I am glad that you went! I know

that you are in heaven with Jesus, experiencing peace and joy. Although, we do miss you so very much.

Reader's Notes

Assignment: Have you ever been bitter? Write about how events have changed you.

What was it? How does it make you feel?

chapter 3

What Am I, Chopped Liver?

Naomi returned ... accompanied by Ruth.

—Ruth 1:22

After Naomi's dramatic return to Bethlehem, she was not by herself. I wonder what Ruth must of thought. I know what I would have: *What am I, chopped liver?* "I left my people and my god to follow you, I swore a devotion to you even unto death and God's judgment upon my life if I ever left you, and I determined not to leave your side (Ruth 1:16–18)." Naomi returned, and she was not empty; Ruth accompanied her (Ruth 1:22).

Ruth was Naomi's daughter-in-law, and she followed her to Bethlehem when the barley harvest began. The Moabite had been married to Naomi's son Chilion for ten years and never bore children (Ruth 1:4). When they heard news of food in Bethlehem, Ruth prepared with Orpah and Naomi for the return trip (Ruth 1:6). Naomi, not Ruth, persuaded Orpah to return (Ruth 1:14), and she declared to Naomi her intent (Ruth 1:16–17).

The author does not give the reader a clue as to what Ruth was thinking after Naomi called herself Mara and made it known to the community that she was bitter, empty, afflicted, and unfortunate (Ruth 1:20–21). She stood by Naomi's side and was not swayed; Ruth never made a scene or declared her presence. Instead, she was silent.

Ruth was submissive and obedient to Naomi (Ruth 2:2–3). She asked for Naomi's permission to glean in the fields, and Naomi granted her request (Ruth 2:2a–2b). Ruth gleaned in the fields of Boaz, who was from the same family as Elimelech, Naomi's deceased husband (Ruth 2:1, 3). Naomi told Ruth to continue in Boaz's fields, and she did (Ruth 2:22). Ruth was not headstrong; she was submissive to Naomi. Her obedience spared her life, and under Boaz's protection, none could touch her (Ruth 2:22). Ruth, who was the sole provider for Naomi, worked in the fields of Boaz until the barley and wheat harvest were finished and stayed with her mother-in-law (Ruth 2:23).

Author's Notes

Although Ruth was not considered important, she was in God's plan when it came to Naomi's life. God was going to use her to restore Naomi. How do I see myself? It's been a long journey, and at times I have wondered if God was near. Was I important to God, or had God forgotten me? The suffering at times just seemed too much.

Reader's Notes

Assignment: Write about yourself. How do you see yourself?

chapter 4

The Saga Continues

Naomi was hopeless. Her circumstances rendered her outside the realm of her social status. Without a husband and sons, she had lost her security and hope of a grandchild to continue her husband's lineage. Naomi finds herself dealing with many losses: She moved from Bethlehem to Moab, leaving behind family and friends. Elimelech, her husband, died. Mahlon, her firstborn son, died. Chilion, her last son, died. Orpah, her daughter-in-law, returned home. And, finally, she left Moab to return to Bethlehem. Naomi believed that the Almighty had caused her bitterness, emptiness, affliction, and unfortunate experiences. In Bethlehem, there was hope of a harvest, so she returned.

Naomi's hope was for much more than food. God's plan included Ruth, her daughter-in-law; the land of Elimelech; the Levirate law; kinsman redeemer Boaz; and God's sovereignty, mercy, grace, and favor.

Author's Notes

Sunday, May 9, 2010, Mother's Day, Thoughts of David

How I miss my son, David, but I celebrate his life, his smile, his noises, his talk, his laughter, and all that he is. David's hands, his quickness—it was like yesterday when he was here in the garden and in the garage with his fiancé, putting together my swing, I remember him driving me to class. I was acting like a backseat driver when I panicked and upset him. I apologized. I was so fragile; he was so fragile.

The thought of my son going to war was prominent. The news pointed to it. I remember the day he came to church and brought the recruiter. I was busy and told him to meet me at home. When I arrived, everyone was gathered around the table. David explained why the recruiter had come that night. He could not join the marines without his parents' consent. We discussed the positives and negatives of his recruitment, and despite it all, we could not persuade David to change his mind. He felt it was time for him to do something before the time got away. He was only seventeen years old. It was set, and we signed.

Before David could get to boot camp, he had to discipline himself. He was so excited. That summer, David worked hard to prepare himself. Fall began, and David lost interest in school and started to get into trouble. He got involved with the wrong group. We knew we had to intervene to keep him busy. We decided that he would attend night school to finish a semester early so that he could enter in the marines after he turned eighteen.

David was disappointed with the outcome of football trials for the varsity team. His decision to leave the team caused hardship on behalf of the coach. He endured and did not give up. He was prepared for the marines.

On February 24, 2003, at four o'clock in the morning, the recruiter came to take David to boot camp. We said our good-byes and knew we would not see him until he graduated from boot camp. Afterward, he would return to walk the stage for his high school graduation.

The phone call came. David had crushed his thumb in the Crucible. He had jumped with an ammo can across a ravine. He was so upset. A decision had to be made: Would he remain in the marines or return home? We had made our plans; the flight, hotel, and car rental were booked. It could all be cancelled if he was not allowed to graduate. We were not disappointed by God. David was permitted to graduate because of his distinction as a marine.

Reader's Notes

Assignment: Write about the loss of your loved one. It might be difficult at first, but just keep trying. Or maybe you don't want to relive it again, and that is okay too.

chapter 5

I Will Cry!

Hopelessness welled up in my heart as I gazed at my bleak situation. What else could happen? In the mornings, depression hit as I stared into the living room from my bedroom with hopes of glimpsing a shadow of my son, who was killed by a drunk driver, only to see nothing but gloom. I waved my hand in hopes that my son or God would wave back, but there was no response.

My son's plan of eight grandchildren and my house next to his so I could take them vanished into thin air on Sunday, August 29, 2004. We heard the knock at the door at four o'clock in the afternoon. I sat up on the couch as my husband opened the door.

We had an unexpected visit from two marines dressed in their blues. Immediately, my mind went back to Fallujah, Iraq, but my son was here in the States.

My son died at two thirty in the morning, not too long after he spoke to his fiancé and his dad. We were assured he did not feel a thing. After the news, I ran to his bedroom, then to my bedroom, and finally to the kitchen. I could not find him or a way of escape through a window.

I found myself on the kitchen floor next to the refrigerator, which was covered with reminders of his homecoming—the writing board with our plans, an email from a friend about my son and well wishes, a picture magnet of him in his blues with his extra chevrons on display. I could not believe it. My only son was gone. How could this be?

In 2008, Memorial Day came again, and the tears of sadness flowed at the tragedy of our son's death. It was so sad that day, I woke up knowing it was different from an ordinary workday. As usual, we went to David's grave and arranged flowers for him and were thanked by a stranger for our son's service to his country. I cried.

The sadness continued for two days until I finally cried again. Usually I like to go to his graveside by myself so I can cry, but on Memorial Day, there were too many people around for expressions of wailing. On Saturday, June 7, 2008, I cried for two days at the loss of my son.

Author's Notes

A good friend told me not to cry. At the time, all I could think to do was cry. I had experienced the greatest loss of my life. All I could feel was the pain and how it would not go away. Why would I not cry? I know she meant well, but I was not going to allow her to stop my tears. Perhaps she didn't want me to hurt anymore. I say cry!

Reader's Notes

Assignment: You have permission to cry. Get it all out. It is okay to cry. Give yourself permission.

chapter 6

God Has a Sense of Humor: Turtles

My husband's sport is fishing. Our whole family enjoys it. When our daughter was little, she would cast her Snoopy fishing rod into the pond and pull out a bream. Thirteen was the last count. David enjoyed fishing with his dad too. We have memories of our last fishing trip before his death; he, his fiancé, my husband, and I went to Fellows Lake.

It was a sunny August day. After the luncheon my department held in our son's honor, we had planned to take the rest of the day to fish. We quickly went home to change and then headed to the lake. The wind was blowing just enough to keep us cool high up on the embankment of the bridge. The water was refreshing in the cove. We could not have asked for a better day for an afternoon of fishing. I remember the picture of the small fish my husband caught that day and his big smile as my son put a worm on his fiancé's hook.

Catch and release! My husband and I practiced that

rule, and every now then he would bring home a turtle. He has such a heart for turtles; my husband loves them. I would always ask, "Now, are you sure it is not a snapping turtle?" and he would assure me, "No, it's not." I wanted to make sure. Reluctantly, I would allow him to bring home his pets.

My garden became the new home of every turtle my husband happened to see while driving home from the lake. I might be exaggerating. At least, that was how it seemed at the time. We placed a small white fence around the garden to make sure they could not escape. In the evenings, we delighted in watching them. My husband had written their names on their backs, all done in love. When my son came home from fighting in Fallujah, Iraq, in 2004, the big news was the new additions to our family: the turtles. "Come and see them. They are here somewhere," my husband said. He wanted to surprise him. I can still see our son's smile as Dad found the turtles. "You have to see them."

Our daughter loves turtles too. I wonder why. She purchased a ceramic turtle to place in her lawn, and we often purchased turtle objects. The turtle lamp we gave her was so cute. Our daughter enjoyed it very much. I think it is in the attic of our home now. Dad brought a pair of turtles from the lake for our daughter. Then he found a little one on the road, and he had to stop and pick it up for our daughter, so that made three. When she came home, she brought the turtles with stickers on their backs with their names to avoid confusion. I wonder where she got that idea. The nursery was my garden, and she would check on them from time to time to make sure they had not escaped. I laughed and said, "God has a sense of humor. I am grandmother to turtles."

Author's Notes

Laugh. It is okay to laugh! I learned to laugh by watching comedy television shows, listening to Christian comedians, and reading funny Christian books. It's hard to laugh when all you can do is grieve, but as you begin to practice, joy comes. I began to hear myself laugh again, and eventually I was on my way to recovery. I had to learn to celebrate my son's life. This took some time to achieve.

Reader's Notes

Assignment: Buy a book that makes you laugh or listen to a Christian comedian or watch a comedy on television. Learn how to laugh again. You can do it. Write about how you experienced laughter again.

chapter 7

Grief Comes in All Shapes and Forms

Naomi experienced grief like others in the Bible. In the Old Testament, Rachel wept for her children. She wanted them even to the point of death (Jer. 31:15–17). David grieved when Absolom was killed, although he threatened his kingdom (2 Sam. 18:33). Job lost everything in an instant; tragedy struck his children when they were gathered together (Job 1:13–20). The news of his children's deaths struck a major blow to his life. The Shunamite woman longed for a son, and Elisha promised that she would have a son, although as a young boy, he had a heatstroke that caused his death (2 Kings 4:18–37).

In the New Testament, Jairus's daughter died, and a grieving father and mother were left with mourners making screeching sounds (Mark 5:38). A widow walked in the processional of her only son while the tears flowed from her worn eyes (Luke 7:11–17). Mary and Martha's brother Lazarus died, and they mourned their loss; many Jews came to console them, but they found no comfort

(John 11:19). Mary, the mother of Jesus, experienced grief as she saw her son on that cross and bloodied, marred beyond recognition. Although she had other sons, she experienced the agony of grief (John 19:25–27).

Author's Notes

Jesus experienced grief when Joseph, his father, died. He was left to take care of his mother and their family business of carpentry.

Reader's Notes

Assignment: What have you experienced? Write about your healing and what it would look like for you.

chapter 8

My Hope

One evening, tears rolled down my cheeks as I lay in bed while my husband stood beside me, comforting me and holding my hand. I stared at my mirrored dresser filled with mementos, gifts from my children's lives, and their gifts to me, including my daughter's porcelain doll that her aunt and uncle gave to her. I have kept it in hopes of giving it to my grandchildren. There was also the *What Mother Took* book, a Mother's Day gift from my son for my birthday. I also saw the set of pomander-scented tea candles he gave me at our last Christmas together.

I lay there in despair. I had felt it before, several years ago. Then I heard the words *Naomi's hope*. This was not the first time I had heard God speak to me. I remembered when I was first saved. Missionaries gladly prayed for me at my local church that I would have boldness to preach the gospel. I was shy and timid, nervous from my childhood well into my teenage years. I would knit all day, and I was never bothered until one day my mother tried to hide my knitting needles. I love you, Mom!

The following week, during lunch, I heard the words, "This is it, and this is the time." At that time, a new employee came into the lounge, but I was the only one there. He came in to eat lunch. I had only been saved for several months and did not know how to witness or know the Roman road to salvation. I knew one thing: if I led him to church, he would be saved. And he did. Jesus saved him. I was amazed! I went to his baptismal service and probably still have a picture of the event in a box in the attic. I think often about how God spoke audibly to me. The words were so clear. I heard them! God answered the missionary's prayer request.

God spoke these simple words: "Naomi's hope." What does it mean? It is something that was just for me. Since that day, I have studied and meditated on those words. I have studied the book of Ruth repeatedly and learned new aspects about that hope. I purchased the story of Ruth on DVD. I have heard others speak on it and have gleaned from it. The night I heard those words, I was comforted by them. God spoke to me in one of the darkest hours of my life when I was without hope.

Author's Notes

"Be still and know that I am God" (Ps. 46:10). Listen.

Reader's Notes

Assignment: God spoke to me, and He can speak to you. Are you ready? How do you listen? Start by simple communication or prayer. It is your turn.

Conclusion: There Has to Be Hope!

As I sat at my desk, editing chapter 1, "Way Too Much Grief!" I had to stop writing because reliving the experience of my son's death was too much to bear. I gazed up at a picture of my son that someone special drew for me and then at another picture of my future son-in-law with my daughter on the other wall, and I said to myself, "There has to be hope!"

There is hope! One day I will see my Lord Jesus face-to-face and all my loved ones who are in his presence. My daughter and future son-in-law will get married even though British law may say otherwise. Why? Because God is involved in my life and He cares.

There is hope! I must believe there is hope. Without it, there is despair. Faith is the opposite of despair, faith in God. He knows the grief I have experienced. I have eternal life, joy, and many blessings to come. I believe it!

I have presented to you the heartfelt stories of Naomi and of myself. We have both lost everything. You may

Dr. Rosita Cantu

have had similar experiences. May this book bring many blessings and comfort to each family through the Holy Spirit. I pray that you will be touched by Jesus, our Lord and Savior. Thank you!

Printed in the United States
By Bookmasters